Finding Mother, Chia and Chao

A Hmong Folktale

Written by Tou Pao Lor
Illustrated by Choua Xiong

First Edition
Paperback ISBN: 978-1-955541-19-0
Hardcover ISBN: 978-1-955541-20-6

Cover and interior design by Ann Aubitz
Illustrated by Choua Xiong

Published by FuzionPress
1250 E 115th Street
Burnsville, MN 55337
fuzionpress.com
612-781-2815

To Mae Lee, Moua Choua, Nou Ting, Douaneng, and Pajzib, also Muaj Kib, Alvin (Tub Ntxhw), Maivyias, and Maivchoo

Preface

A long time ago, the Hmong did not have any written language. They remembered important events by using oral histories, telling them from one generation to the next. This was the only way Hmong stories were passed on to Hmong children.

I learned this story, *Finding Mother, Chia And Chao*, while I was living in Chiang Kham Refugee Camp in 1991. It was told by an elderly Hmong man living in Thailand. After I learned this story, I would tell it to my little brother and his friends. All the children loved the story very much. While studying at Century College in 1998, I realized this folklore story was very special. I then moved my hand and pen and wrote it down so everyone could read it.

This story about Chia and Chao explains some of the historical background of the Hmong when they still lived in China and had to face life-threatening execution from their Chinese enemies. This story also exhibits a little of the Hmong cultural beliefs and why most modern Hmong still follow and practice our traditions today. For example, whenever we have a ceremony, and the food is cooked, we invite the souls of our parents who have already died to come and eat first. We ask them to protect and bless us. We then eat later by setting a new table of food.

4 long time ago, there was a husband named Ta Khoua Toua (*Ntaj Qhuas Ntuam*), who had a wife named Gao Shay (*Nkauj Seb*) and two sons. The first son was named Chia (*Ntshiab*), and the second son was named Chao (*Ntshaus*). They were a Hmong family who lived in a village in China. In this village, Ta Khoua Toua was the leader of many Hmong families. Every day, people in the village would go to work in the field early in the morning and then return home when the sky was getting dark. Children would play and run around with their friends and siblings happily like bunnies. Farm animals were everywhere in the back and front yards, grazing calmly. People in the village had lived peacefully for many hundreds of years with their neighbors.

While Chia and Chao were still very little, the Chinese waged war on all Hmong villages in China. There was great chaos in Ta Khoua Toua's family's village. The Chinese wanted to kill and wipe out all Hmong in China. Although all villagers were informed that the Chinese were coming with many soldiers to attack them, Ta Khoua Toua never felt afraid to fight them.

When the Chinese soldiers arrived at the Hmong village, many Hmong men took their families and ran away. Many other Hmong men in the village stood up and helped Ta Khoua Toua fight against their enemies to keep their village and protect their families. Unfortunately, the Chinese soldiers completely wiped out Ta Khoua Toua and all his men who had stayed behind. The only men who survived were those who had escaped before the Chinese arrived. The rest of the survivors were women and children.

After Gao Shay found that Ta Khoua Toua was killed, she was very afraid that the Chinese soldiers would someday kill her two sons, Chia and Chao. One day, she secretly took Chia and Chao to hide in a big cave far from the village, hoping the Chinese soldiers could never find them. Gao Shay brought Chia and Chao a big basket of uncooked rice and a big basket of raw corn. When Gao Shay left Chia and Chao in the cave to get some more food and their possessions, she was captured by the Chinese soldiers.

When the Chinese knew they had killed all the Hmong men in the village, they started ransacking peoples' houses and killing every little boy. However, the Chinese did not kill all the women and the little girls because the Chinese soldiers needed them to be their slaves. Thus, Gao Shay and many women and girls became slaves to the Chinese.

Chia and Chao waited day after day for their mother to return to the cave, but she never returned. Chia and Chao ate only uncooked rice and raw corn. Many years passed, and their rice and corn were all eaten. When they had nothing to eat, they would leave the cave to find edible plants and tree roots to stop their hunger.

Many more years passed, and the people who had escaped during the attack of the Chinese soldiers started to return to the village. They cut trees to build houses and do their farm work again. Finally, the farmers' fields reached the big cave where Chia and Chao lived.

When Chia and Chao saw Hmong people working in their fields, they left the cave and became friends with those people. Chia and Chao started to make a living by working for any Hmong farmers who would hire them. Every day and night, Chia and Chao worked very hard to earn a little bit of money. After Chia and Chao saved enough money to build themselves a house, they both found wives to marry. Chia and Chao each had a few sons.

Every day, Chia and Chao told their sons to pasture the animals and bring them back to their pens in the evening. One day when the children and the sheep and goats arrived on the mountain, the animals suddenly spoke and said, "Little boys, every day when we arrive on the mountain, we go and find our own grass to eat. However, today after arriving on the mountain, we felt too tired to get our own food. Would you boys please get us some grass to eat, and then we will sing you a song?" The children agreed to get the sheep and the goats some grass to eat. After they finished eating, the children asked the animals to sing them a song as they had promised.

The sheep and the goats said, "Okay!" and then they sang:
    May ay - may ay - long lay,
    flowers are fully blossoming on mountains!
If Chia and Chao do not go
to find the old Chinese slave lady to come
and teach them the cultural tradition,
then the two of them will die!

May ay - may ay - long lay,
flowers are blooming to fill in all of the ravines!
If Chia and Chao do not go
to find the old Chinese slave lady to come
and teach them the cultural tradition,
then the two of them and their offspring will die!

The sheep and the goats asked the children, "Little boys, have you already learned the song?" The children answered, "No, it was a very good song, but we have not learned it yet." The sheep and the goats said, "If you still have not learned it, we will be very pleased to sing it again." After repeating the song, the sheep and the goats asked the boys again, "Boys, did you learn and remember it now?" The children answered that they could remember and had learned it. The sky was getting dark, and the children had to take the animals back home.

After arriving home, the children told Chia and Chao what had happened while taking the sheep and goats to the pasture. When Chia and Chao heard what the children told them, they were very surprised and did not believe the story. They quickly said, "What kind of sheep and goats would know how to talk and sing? Something bad will soon happen to them." Then Chia and Chao asked the children, "What did the sheep and the goats say?" The children told Chia and Chao the song they heard and learned from the sheep and goats.

4fter hearing the song from their children, Chia and Chao said, "Really! You little boys are liars." The children again said, "This really was what the sheep and the goats sang." Chia and Chao were not sure what to believe and said, "There is something bad happening to those sheep and goats. They all might soon die!" A dog was sitting in the house, and it suddenly answered, "Fathers, that was true. I also heard that." Chia and Chao said, "Uh, what kind of dog is that? Why would it speak?!" Chia and Chao picked up a big wooden door latch and hit the dog with it. The wooden door latch hurt the dog, and the dog suddenly groaned, "Wau, wau!" It then ran away.

A cat, who was coming from a corner of the house, laughed, "Ha, ha! Every day that dog tries to make trouble for me and hurt me. See, now it has been hit with a big wooden door latch by the grandfathers." When Chia and Chao heard the cat talk, they angrily said, "Uh, this cat might want to die because it also talked!" Chia and Chao got a rod and hit the cat with it. The cat was hurt and cried, "Meow, meow," and then ran away. A trembling mouse came, and it squeaked, "Ha, ha! Every day and night, that cat loves to trap me in every corner hole and try to catch me. Tonight, the grandfathers used the rod to hurt it, so it then cried 'Meow, meow.'" Chia and Chao sighed and said, "Uh, this mouse also wants to die, or why would it also speak?" Then Chia and Chao used a chili pepper pestle to hit the mouse. The mouse was hurt and quickly ran away. The pestle groaned immediately and said, "Fathers, please do not hurt me this bad. My ribs are really aching!"

After hearing and seeing these odd events, Chia and Chao felt frustrated and were not motivated to make a living. They were exhausted and did not even want to care for the family. Every day, instead of working on the farms, Chia and Chao would see a Hmong and a Chinese fortuneteller about the mysterious problem.

The two fortunetellers opened a book and read it again and again and said, "Oh! Heaven, Chia, and Chao, if you two expect to have a healthy family, you need to go to where a Chinese merchant will sell some old Chinese slave ladies and buy one. However, do not buy someone that is too expensive or too cheap. Please buy the one the Chinese merchants would sell for thirteen silver coins. She will be the one who will be able to teach you two how to practice the cultural tradition that the sheep and the goats sang about."

Chia and Chao returned home after learning everything from the fortunetellers. They prepared money and rice to find the old Chinese slave lady. Once everything was prepared, Chia and Chao walked out their door and began their journey.

After a few days, they reached a Chinese city. They went into a shop and asked a Chinese man, "Do you have any old Chinese slave ladies for sale?" The Chinese man said, "We had a very old and dirty woman sitting over in the corner there. You two can come in and take a look." Chia and Chao asked, "How much does she cost?" "Fifteen silver coins," the Chinese man said. Chia and Chao realized she was too expensive, so they left.

C hia and Chao found a different Chinese family and asked, "Do you have some old Chinese slave ladies for sale?" That Chinese family said, "Yes, we do have a few. We sell each for seven silver coins." They pretended she was too expensive because she was not the right person they sought. It wasn't easy to find the one described by the two fortunetellers; Chia and Chao felt like giving up.

Chia and Chao arrived in a new Chinese city one day later. They went to a Chinese merchant and asked, "Do you have any old Chinese slave ladies for sale? We want to buy one." The Chinese merchant answered, "Yes, we used to have a lot, but all were sold. There is a dirty and ugly one left over there." Chia and Chao went in to take a look and asked for the price. "Thirteen silver coins," said the Chinese merchant. When Chia and Chao heard the price was right, they quickly said, "We will buy her! We will buy her!" Chia and Chao paid the Chinese merchant and took the old Chinese slave lady with them.

After making the purchase, Chia and Chao killed a few chickens and cooked brand-new sticky rice for lunch on the way home. Chia and Chao ground up some hot peppers and cooked the old Chinese slave lady a humble meal of corn for lunch. They left the Chinese city and returned home.

After a long day walking home, they came to a small river. It was about noon, and time for them to have lunch. They stopped on the river bank. Chia and Chao said, "Old Chinese slave lady, we will have lunch here for a while. Would you please walk down there a little bit to have your lunch because you are such a dirty, ugly, disgusting, and bad-smelling person?" The old Chinese slave lady quietly answered, "Okay, I will move down there." She slowly walked down along the riverside to have lunch while Chia and Chao ate beside the river.

Chia and Chao quickly tore their cooked chickens into little pieces and opened their brand-new cooked sticky rice to eat. After Chia and Chao had finished, Chia said, "Chao, Chao, would you please go down there to see if the old Chinese slave lady has finished eating her lunch? If she has not finished yet, tell her to hurry, or we will be late getting home." Chao quickly walked down there and said, "Old Chinese slave lady, did you have your lunch?" Chao did not hear the old Chinese slave lady answer. He did not know if she had eaten her lunch or not. Then Chao saw the old Chinese slave lady crying and groaning.

She was staring toward a high cliff where there was a big cave. The old Chinese slave lady cried and said:

"Oh, heaven! This is the place where my
dearest husband, Ta Khoua Toua, used to look
after his cows and where I, Gao Shay, used
to winnow and blow away the husk of the rice. Also,
it was the place where I used to feed my chickens!

Why, this is the place where my dearest husband
Ta Khoua Toua used to look after his horses
and where I, Gao Shay, used to blow the
husk of the rice. Also, it is the place where
I used to feed my pigs. There is the big cave
where I hid my two sons, Chia and Chao.

Now they might have already become the food
and stool of tigers. I am now already very old
and just waiting to die. Why today do I have
this chance to walk onto this scene?!"

The old Chinese slave lady again cried and looked at the big cave. When Chao heard what the old Chinese slave lady sang, he quickly returned to where Chia was eating. Chao said, "Chia, Chia, I do not know if the old Chinese slave lady ate her lunch. But when I got there, I saw she was crying, staring at that big cave, and singing a song." Then Chao told Chia what the old slave lady had sung. Chia thought awhile and said, "Chao, maybe she is our mother, Gao Shay!"

Chia and Chao hurried back to where the old Chinese slave lady was and asked, "Old Chinese slave lady, you said you have two sons and hid them in that big cave. What did you give your sons to eat inside the big cave?" She said, "A long time ago, the Chinese waged war on our Hmong village where my family lived. The Chinese arrived and killed all the men, including my husband, Ta Khoua Toua. Moreover, they killed every single boy. They left only the women and girls to take home to be their slaves. I was very afraid that they would kill my two sons, so I hid them in that big cave before the Chinese started killing all the little boys. I got my two sons a big basket of uncooked rice and a big basket of raw corn to eat there. The older brother was named Chia, and the little brother was named Chao. I was caught when I returned to the village to get some food and some of my family's possessions. Then the Chinese soldiers took me to be enslaved until today."

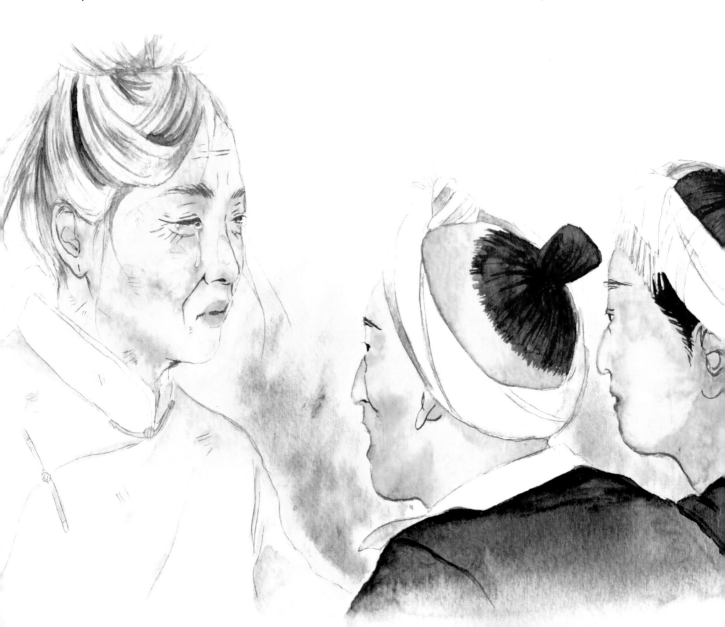

Chia quickly said, "I am Chia, and he is Chao. He is my little brother." The old Chinese slave lady excitedly said, "If you two are Chia and Chao, please show me your feet. I want to look at your feet because before leaving Chia and Chao in the big cave, I used a knife to make a scar on one of Chao's big toes. I cut a little mark on Chia's sole. Please let me see your feet to see if they have any scars." Chia and Chao showed their feet to the old Chinese slave lady. She saw that on Chia's sole was a scar there, and there was also a scar on Chao's big toe.

Suddenly Chia, Chao, and the old Chinese slave lady cried and hugged each other tightly. While crying, Chia and Chao said, "Mother, if you are not our mother, whose mother would you be?" The old Chinese slave lady cried and said, "Oh, heaven, Chia and Chao! If you two are not my sons, whose sons would you be?" The three of them cried hard, especially the old slave lady. She groaned and groaned.

Chia and Chao found their mother a comfortable place to sit and gave her their brand-new cooked sticky rice and cooked chicken to eat. After their mother was full, Chia asked Chao to go home first to boil some warm water to bathe their mother because she was too dirty, torn, and disgusting. Chia would take their mother home slowly because she was old and could not walk fast.

After arriving, Chia and Chao told their mother to change her clothes and helped her bathe. After bathing, Chia and Chao gave their mother new clothes to wear. They were pleased that their mother and her sons could finally be reunited after many years.

4 A few days later, Chia and Chao's mother asked Chia and Chao's wives to help wash her dirty clothes. She said, "Daughter-in-law Chia and Daughter-in-law Chao, I have some very dirty, torn, and disgusting clothes over there. I would like the two of you to help me wash them. However, please do not be disgusted by them, although they are disgusting. I will give my Daughter-in-law Chia the skirt and the belt. I will give my Daughter-in-law Chao the shirt and the apron. Again, please do not feel disgusted. There are knots I made in the clothes to keep things. Each of you needs to take a pair of scissors and cut every single knot that you see. Whatever you find inside, you can keep."

Chia's wife felt very uncomfortable washing the clothes, so she said, "Sister-in-law Chao, although she is our mother, I feel very disgusted by those clothes. If you wash the clothes you were asked to wash, please take mine with you to wash, too. I really feel uncomfortable washing them."

Chao's wife did not say anything. She used a stick to pick the clothes up from the ground and put them into her basket. She took a pair of scissors with her, then left for the small river where they usually went to wash their clothes and get water. While Chao's wife was washing the clothes, she saw many knots that were all tied tightly. She used the scissors to cut off every knot. While cutting them from the clothes, she saw each knot had a silver coin, which she took. After cutting the skirt, the shirt, and the apron, she had a big basket full of silver coins.

When Chao's wife was washing and cutting the knots, Chia's wife came to the river to get some water. Chia's wife saw Chao's wife had many silver coins in the basket. She then said, "Oh! Sister-in-law Chao, how come you have so much money?" Chao's wife answered, "Mother asked us to wash her clothes. She also told us to take a pair of scissors and cut whatever knots we saw and keep whatever we found. Maybe you did not have the good fortune of getting this money because of the feeling you had toward the clothes.

There is still one piece left over there that you can wash. Also, you can keep what you find. I already washed three pieces of clothing, and I think this money is enough for me." Chia's wife said, "Ah! Sister-in-law Chao, please share with me some money, okay!" Chao's wife did not share the money with Chia's wife, and then she returned home. Chia's wife got the left-over piece of belt washed, and she got about a bowl full of money. She cried and did not feel happy.

When Chia's wife got home, she told Chia and Chao's mother that Chao's wife did not share her money. The mother said, "My dear Daughter-in-law Chia and my dear Daughter-in-law Chao, because I did not want the two of you to feel upset, I decided to give each of you two pieces of clothes to wash. I also told you two to take a pair of scissors and cut whatever knots you saw and take whatever you saw. Fortune did not shine on you, so do not feel sad." Then Chia's wife cried again.

One day, Chia and Chao each brought a chair and sat near their mother, Gao Shay. Their mother said, "Oh! Heaven, Chia, and Chao! Why did you two come to find your mother?" Chia and Chao described all the mysterious things that had happened to them and asked their mother to tell them what was happening. The mother said, "My dearest sons, you two must kill a chicken or a pig and cook rice. Once everything is well cooked, set up a table and put the food on it. Get a chair and put it in the front of the table, and then older brother Chia will invite the spirit of your father, Ta Khoua Toua, to come and sit there. You two should sit on the opposite side of the table and then give the spirit of your father a spoon to eat with.

W hile inviting your father to eat, ask him to come and protect and bless you two and all your family members. This is the main reason that I must come and teach the two of you how to practice the cultural traditions and pass them to the future generation." Chia and Chao started to prepare as directed by their mother.

From that day on, Chia and Chao had a peaceful life through the days and nights with their mother, wives, and children. Every year the family harvested enough food to feed the family and was able to save some seeds for the coming year. Their food storage bins were completely filled. House animals were once again roaming in the back and front yards. Children and grandchildren were also running and playing happily with each other like bunnies again.

Chia and Chao's wives and daughters would sit in a circle and embroider their clothes with floral designs. In the evening, Chia, Chao, and their sons would talk about getting ready for the field the following morning and taking the sheep and goats to pasture in the mountain. Their calm and smiling faces were so peaceful. Every time Chia and Chao celebrated ceremonies, they would never forget to invite their father Ta Khoua Toua's spirit to enjoy the celebration and to bless them.

Author: Dr. Tou Pao Lor

Pictured: Chiang Kham Refugee Camp, 1990.

Tou Pao Lor is a Hmong refugee who was born in Laos in 1971. In May 1979, his father and three children, including Tou, fled from Laos to Thailand because of the Secret War. His mother, second older sister, and younger brother died during their escape. After arriving in the refugee camp, his father did not want to make resettlement plans to any foreign country because he hoped that they would soon be able to return to a peaceful Laos. His father wanted to remain in the camp as long as they could. They lived in three refugee camps in Thailand for sixteen years: Ban Vinai, Chiang Kham, and Phanat Nikhom. While living in the camps, Tou studied Thai, Lao, Hmong, and Chinese for about six years. He also studied English.

His family finally arrived in Saint Paul, Minnesota, in 1995, when he was about 24 years old and married with two children. He went to an adult school named Hubbs Center for Lifelong Learning to study English and received his adult high school diploma in six months. Going to school as an adult learner was an uphill battle for him, but he made it. In 2012 he completed his doctoral degree in education and leadership from Saint Mary's University of Minnesota in the Twin Cities. Since then, he has been a psychotherapist in the Hmong and Karen communities.

He is writing a few books on his life experiences in Laos, refugee camps in Thailand, and his time in the United States. He likes writing and recording for his family, and he hopes his stories will encourage people to record their life experiences. He remembers the happiness of being together in the village, refugee camp, and the United States, the sadness of leaving, and the joy of reunions that his family has experienced.

Illustrator: Choua Xiong is a freelance illustrator based in the Midwest. She previously illustrated a children's book with Hmong Educational Resources Publisher, *Puag Thaum Ub: Hmoob Xeem*. Choua's primary goal as an illustrator is to help others bring their story to life with the stroke of her brush and vivid imagination.

Acknowledgments

To the respected Hmong gentleman grandfather, whose name is unknown: Thanks for coming from a Hmong village in Thailand to the edge of Chiang Kham Refugee Camp to share this beautiful folk story with your camp's Hmong refugee fellows. This is a beautiful historical and cultural folklore story of the Hmong people. This story will stay deep inside the hearts and minds of the Hmong community for a long time. I was very fortunate to have had the opportunity to obtain this cassette recording while you were in the camp telling the story.

To Hmong boys and girls in the community: I encourage you to ask your parents or grandparents to tell you a Hmong folklore story when they have time and when you have the opportunity. We can set aside time to interact with our parents and grandparents and ask them about their past lives. Folklore stories tell us many wonderful things, such as history about our roots, culture, values, and who we are. If we do not record these stories while our elders are alive, they will be gone forever.

To my children: When Daddy was still little like you, Daddy and his friends would sit in a small group and take turns telling stories, one after another. Almost every night, we would ask elders to tell us folklore stories. We would sit around a fireplace and quietly listen. Please visit your grandpa and grandma soon and ask them to tell you a story. They are waiting for you to ask, "Grandpa and Grandma, please tell me a folklore story."